LOVE

BEYOND

Pain

A COMPASSIONATE GUIDE TO SUPPORTING A PARTNER THROUGH TRAUMA

'EZEKIEL AGBOOLA

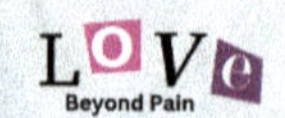

INTRODUCTION

Few threads in the fabric of human relationships are as complicated and delicate as those weaved from traumatic events. This book, "Love Beyond Pain," is the result of a deep awareness and recognition of the specific obstacles that people encounter when they love someone who has experienced trauma. Its purpose is multifaceted, aiming to illuminate the path for partners who find themselves entangled in the shadows of their loved one's past traumas. This book seeks to be a beacon of hope, a wellspring of understanding, and a practical guide for those who are determined to maintain and nurture their relationships despite the storms of past hurts.

Loving someone with a traumatic past can feel like navigating a labyrinth. The twists and turns, the unexpected triggers, and the deep-seated fears can create an environment where confusion and frustration easily take root. Many partners feel ill-equipped to handle the complexities that arise, often finding themselves at a loss for how to provide the necessary support without losing themselves in the process. This book aims to fill that gap by offering both a deep understanding of trauma and practical strategies to foster a supportive and resilient relationship. It is crafted with empathy and insight, recognizing that every the relationship is unique, and there is no one-size-fits-all solution. Instead, it offers a variety of tools and perspectives, allowing readers to tailor the advice to their specific circumstances.

The ultimate goal of this book is to help partners see beyond the immediate behaviours and symptoms of trauma to the person they love, understanding the root causes and learning how to navigate the complex dynamics that trauma introduces into a relationship. By providing a comprehensive understanding of trauma, its effects, and the healing process, this book aims to empower partners to support their loved ones effectively while also taking care of their own emotional well-being. It is about fostering a relationship that is not defined by trauma but strengthened by the resilience and love that can emerge when both partners commit to understanding and Love Beyond Pain.

To support a partner with a traumatic past, one must first understand what trauma is and how it manifests in behavior and relationships. Trauma is a deeply distressing or disturbing experience that overwhelms an individual's ability to cope, leaving them feeling helpless and vulnerable. It can stem from various sources, including childhood abuse, sexual assault, domestic violence, natural disasters, and combat experiences, among others. The impact of trauma is profound and multifaceted, affecting not only the individual's mental and emotional health but also their physical well-being and interpersonal relationships.

Trauma changes the way the brain processes information and perceives threats. For many individuals, traumatic experiences are stored in their minds and bodies in a way that makes them persistently feel as though they are in danger, even in safe situations. This heightened state of arousal can lead to a range of symptoms, including anxiety, depression, hypervigilance, flashbacks, and dissociation. Understanding these symptoms and their origins is crucial for partners who wish to provide meaningful support. It is not enough to recognize that a partner is struggling; one must also understand the underlying mechanisms that drive their behavior and emotions.

The effects of trauma on relationships are significant and often challenging. Trust, communication, and intimacy can all be impacted by a partner's traumatic experiences. For instance, a person who has experienced betrayal or abuse may find it difficult to trust others, even those who genuinely care for them. They might be hyper-aware of potential threats, misinterpreting neutral or positive actions as dangerous. This can lead to misunderstandings, conflicts, and a sense of distance in the relationship. Additionally, trauma can affect a person's ability to regulate their emotions, resulting in mood swings, anger, or withdrawal, which can further strain the relationship. Understanding trauma is not just about recognizing its symptoms but also about appreciating its pervasive impact on every aspect of a person's life. It requires a compassionate and non-judgmental approach, recognizing that the behaviors and reactions that can be most challenging to deal with are often the result of deep-seated pain and fear. By developing a thorough understanding of trauma, partners can begin to see beyond the surface behaviors to the underlying struggles their loved ones face. This understanding is the foundation upon which effective support and healing can be built.

Hope and Healing

Despite the significant challenges that trauma introduces into relationships, there is a profound potential for hope and healing. The journey is not easy, and it requires patience, commitment, and resilience from both partners. However, it is entirely possible to maintain a healthy, loving relationship even in the presence of past trauma. In fact, many couples find that the process of navigating these challenges together deepens their bond and strengthens their connection. Healing from trauma is a multifaceted process that involves both individual and relational work. For the person who has experienced trauma, this often means engaging in therapy or counseling to address the underlying issues and develop healthier coping mechanisms. Professional help is crucial because trauma can be deeply ingrained, and its effects are not always easily overcome without expert guidance. Therapy can provide a safe space for individuals to process their experiences, understand their triggers, and learn new ways of relating to themselves and others.

For the partner, supporting a loved one through their healing journey involves a combination of empathy, patience, and practical strategies. It means being willing to listen without judgment, to validate their partner's experiences and feelings, and to offer consistent support and reassurance. It also means educating oneself about trauma and its effects, so as to better understand and respond to their partner's needs. Importantly, it involves recognizing and respecting one's own limits, ensuring that the partner also engages in self-care and seeks support when needed.

One of the most important aspects of maintaining a healthy relationship amidst trauma is building a foundation of trust and safety. This involves creating an environment where both partners feel secure and valued, and where open and honest communication is encouraged. It requires a commitment to working through conflicts constructively, recognizing that disagreements and misunderstandings are a normal part of any relationship. By approaching these challenges with compassion and a willingness to understand each other's perspectives, couples can navigate the difficulties that arise and emerge stronger on the other side. Hope in the context of trauma and relationships is not about expecting a quick fix or a perfect outcome. Instead, it is about believing in the possibility of growth and healing, even in the face of significant challenges. It is about recognizing the resilience and strength that both partners bring to the relationship and the potential for love and connection to flourish even in difficult circumstances. This book aims to provide readers with the tools and insights they need to cultivate this hope and to embark on a journey of Love Beyond Pain, building a relationship that is defined not by the trauma they have faced but by the love and resilience they share.

The Journey Ahead

As we embark on this journey together, it is important to acknowledge that every relationship and every individual is unique. Trauma experiences andpaths to healing are diverse, and what works for one couple may not work for another. This book is not a definitive answer but rather a guide that offers a variety of perspectives and strategies, allowing readers to find what resonates with them and their specific situations. It is a companion on the journey, offering support, insight, and encouragement along the way.

In the chapters that follow, we will delve deeper into the nature of trauma, its effects on behavior and relationships, and the specific strategies that can help couples navigate these challenges. We will explore the importance of communication, empathy, and trust, and offer practical advice for building a supportive and resilient relationship. We will also address the critical issue of self-care, recognizing that supporting a partner with a traumatic past can be emotionally demanding and that both partners need to prioritize their own well-being.

Throughout this book, you will find real-life stories and testimonials from individuals and couples who have faced similar challenges. These stories are meant to provide insight and inspiration, showing that it is possible to navigate the complexities of trauma and maintain a loving and healthy relationship. They are a reminder that you are not alone on this journey and that there is a community of individuals who understand and share your struggles. In a broader sense, "Love Beyond Pain" is a testament to the power of love, resilience, and hope. It is an invitation to embark on a journey of understanding, support, and healing, recognizing that even in the presence of trauma, there is the potential for deep and meaningful connection. By approaching this journey with empathy, patience, and an open heart, you can build a relationship that not only survives but thrives in the face of the shadows of the past.

CHAPTER ONE
Understanding Trauma

Trauma is a deeply distressing or disturbing experience that can overwhelm an individual's ability to cope, causing feelings of helplessness and a diminished sense of self. It affects people in numerous ways, influencing their emotional, psychological, and physical well-being. Understanding trauma requires a nuanced approach, recognizing that it is not just the event itself but also the individual's response to it that defines the traumatic experience. Trauma can be in three forms; physical, emotional, psychological.

Physical Trauma

Physical trauma refers to bodily injuries resulting from accidents, violence, or other external forces. These injuries can range from minor cuts and bruises to severe wounds that require extensive medical treatment. The physical effects of trauma are often visible and tangible, making them easier to identify and address. However, the impact of physical trauma goes beyond the immediate physical damage, potentially leading to long-term health issues and emotional distress.

- **Acute Physical Trauma:** This type involves sudden and severe injuries, such as those sustained in car accidents, falls, or physical assaults. Acute physical trauma often necessitates emergency medical care and can have lasting effects on an individual's physical and mental health.

- **Chronic Physical Trauma:** This involves repetitive injuries over time, such as those experienced by victims of domestic violence or individuals in physically demanding jobs. Chronic trauma can lead to ongoing pain, disability, and psychological issues, including anxiety and depression.

Emotional Trauma

Emotional trauma arises from events or experiences that cause intense emotional pain and distress. Unlike physical trauma, the effects of emotional trauma are not always visible but can be equally, if not more, debilitating. Emotional trauma can result from a wide range of experiences, from personal losses and relationship issues to witnessing or being involved in violent incidents.

- **Acute Emotional Trauma:** This type occurs in response to a single, overwhelming event, such as the sudden death of a loved one, a natural disaster, or a severe accident. The intensity of the emotional pain can lead to immediate reactions like shock, denial, and extreme sadness or anger.

- **Chronic Emotional Trauma:** This involves prolonged exposure to distressing situations, such as ongoing abuse, neglect, or living in a war zone. Chronic emotional trauma can erode an individual's sense of safety and stability, leading to long-term emotional and psychological issues.

Psychological Trauma

Psychological trauma, often interwoven with emotional trauma, affects the mind and can alter an individual's cognitive processes and mental health. It results from events that challenge one's perception of the world as a safe and predictable place, leaving deep psychological scars.

- **Acute Psychological Trauma:** Similar to emotional trauma, this type arises from a single distressing event that overwhelms an individual's ability to cope. Examples include experiencing or witnessing a violent crime, being involved in a serious accident, or enduring a sudden life-threatening situation.

- **Complex Psychological Trauma:** This type, also known as complex PTSD, results from exposure to multiple traumatic events over time, often of an interpersonal nature. It can arise from ongoing abuse, neglect, or exposure to repeated traumatic experiences. Complex psychological trauma can profoundly affect an individual's personality, relationships, and overall mental health.

Symptoms and Effects

Trauma manifests in a variety of symptoms, affecting individuals differently based on their personal history, resilience, and support systems. The symptoms of trauma can be broadly categorized into emotional, psychological, and physical effects, each contributing to the overall impact on an individual's life.

Emotional Symptoms and Effects

Emotional symptoms of trauma can vary widely, from intense feelings of sadness and grief to overwhelming anger and fear. These symptoms can persist long after the traumatic event has passed, significantly affecting an individual's quality of life.

- *Anxiety and Fear:* Many trauma survivors experience persistent anxiety and fear, often triggered by reminders of the traumatic event. This can lead to a constant state of hypervigilance, where the individual is always on edge, expecting danger at any moment.

- *Depression and Hopelessness:* Trauma can lead to profound feelings of sadness, hopelessness, and depression. Individuals may struggle to find joy in activities they once enjoyed, feeling disconnected from themselves and others.

- *Anger and Irritability:* Intense and often uncontrollable anger can be a common response to trauma. This anger may be directed outward at others or inward at oneself, leading to conflicts in relationships and a diminished sense of self-worth.

- *Guilt and Shame:* Survivors of trauma often experience guilt and shame, feeling as though they are to blame for what happened to them. This can lead to a pervasive sense of unworthiness and self-loathing.

- *Emotional Numbness:* In an attempt to protect themselves from the pain of their trauma, some individuals may become emotionally numb, detaching themselves from their feelings and from those around them. This can lead to difficulties in forming and maintaining relationships.

Psychological Symptoms and Effects

Psychological symptoms of trauma can significantly alter an individual's thinking patterns, memory, and overall mental health. These symptoms often intersect with emotional symptoms, compounding the challenges faced by trauma survivors.

- *Intrusive Thoughts and Flashbacks:* Many individuals with trauma experience intrusive thoughts and flashbacks, where they relive the traumatic event as if it were happening again. Sensory reminders can trigger these or occur spontaneously, causing intense distress.

- *Nightmares and Sleep Disturbances:* Trauma often disrupts sleep, leading to nightmares and insomnia. The lack of restful sleep can exacerbate other symptoms, creating a vicious cycle of distress and exhaustion.

- *Difficulty Concentrating:* Trauma can impair cognitive functions, making it difficult for individuals to focus, concentrate, or remember things. This can affect their performance at work or school and hinder daily activities.

- *Avoidance Behaviors:* To cope with distressing memories and emotions, trauma survivors may engage in avoidance behaviours, steering clear of places, people, or activities that remind them of the trauma. While this can provide temporary relief, it often leads to isolation and restricts their lives.

- *Dissociation:* Dissociation is a psychological response where individuals feel detached from their bodies or surroundings, as though they are observing themselves from outside. This can be a protective mechanism in response to overwhelming stress but can lead to significant disruptions in daily life.

Physical Symptoms and Effects

Trauma affects not only the mind and emotions but also the body. The physical symptoms of trauma can be direct, such as injuries from a traumatic event, or indirect, resulting from the chronic stress and anxiety that trauma induces.

- *Chronic Pain and Fatigue:* Many trauma survivors experience chronic pain, which can stem from physical injuries or manifest as somatic symptoms related to psychological distress. Fatigue is also common, often exacerbated by sleep disturbances and the ongoing stress of managing trauma symptoms.

- *Headaches and Migraines:* Persistent headaches and migraines are frequent among trauma survivors, linked to the chronic stress and tension they endure.

- *Digestive Issues:* Trauma can affect the digestive system, leading to problems such as irritable bowel syndrome (IBS), nausea, and other gastrointestinal issues. These symptoms are often related to the body's perpetually activated fight-or-flight response.

- *Cardiovascular Problems:* The constant state of heightened arousal and stress can strain the cardiovascular system, increasing the risk of hypertension, heart disease, and other related health issues.

- *Immune System Suppression:* Chronic stress from trauma can weaken the immune system, making individuals more susceptible to infections and illnesses.

The long-term effects of trauma can permeate every aspect of an individual's life, influencing their mental, emotional, and physical well-being. These effects can persist for years, shaping their interactions with others and their overall quality of life.

Trauma can profoundly affect an individual's relationships, often creating barriers to intimacy and trust. The long-term effects of trauma on relationships can manifest in several ways:

- *Trust Issues:* Trauma, especially when it involves betrayal, can make it difficult for individuals to trust others. They may struggle to believe in the reliability and sincerity of others, leading to strained and superficial relationships.

- *Attachment Difficulties:* Trauma can disrupt an individual's ability to form secure attachments. They may either become overly dependent on their partners or remain emotionally distant, unable to engage in the relationship fully.

- *Communication Challenges:* Trauma survivors often find it difficult to communicate their needs and feelings effectively. They may fear being misunderstood or judged, leading to misunderstandings and conflicts.

- *Intimacy Problems:* Trauma, particularly of a sexual nature, can affect an individual's ability to engage in intimate relationships. They may experience fear, discomfort, or disinterest in physical intimacy, impacting their romantic relationships.

The long-term psychological effects of trauma can lead to a range of mental health issues, including:

- *Post-Traumatic Stress Disorder (PTSD):* PTSD is a common long-term effect of trauma, characterized by persistent re-experiencing of the traumatic event, avoidance of trauma-related stimuli, negative changes in mood and cognition, and hyperarousal symptoms.

- *Complex PTSD (C-PTSD):* This condition arises from prolonged exposure to trauma, often involving interpersonal relationships. It includes the symptoms of PTSD along with

The long-term physical effects of trauma can lead to chronic health issues, including:

- *Chronic Pain and Somatic Symptoms:* Persistent physical pain, often with no apparent medical cause, can be a long-term effect of trauma. These somatic symptoms are manifestations of the body's response to ongoing psychological distress.

- *Cardiovascular Disease:* The chronic stress associated with trauma can increase the risk of heart disease, hypertension, and other cardiovascular conditions.

- *Respiratory Issues:* Trauma can affect the respiratory system, leading to conditions such as asthma, chronic obstructive pulmonary disease (COPD), and other breathing difficulties.

- *Metabolic Disorders:* The stress and anxiety from trauma can disrupt metabolic processes, increasing the risk of diabetes, obesity, and other metabolic disorders.

- *Immune System Dysfunction:* The prolonged activation of the body's stress response can weaken the immune system, making individuals more susceptible to infections and chronic illnesses.

Understanding trauma in all its forms and effects is the first step toward healing and helping a partner who has been through it. Trauma is a complicated and varied event that has lasting effects on the mind, body, and spirit.

Recognizing the many forms of trauma, as well as the vast spectrum of symptoms and long-term impacts they can cause, allows us to address them with the empathy, compassion, and understanding needed to help our loved ones and ourselves.

CHAPTER TWO

Recognizing Trauma in Your Partner

Understanding trauma is the first step, but recognizing its presence in your partner is crucial for providing the support they need. This chapter focuses on identifying the signs and indicators of trauma in a partner, as well as understanding the common behaviors that may stem from traumatic experiences. By becoming more attuned to these signs, partners can approach their relationships with greater empathy, patience, and effectiveness. Trauma can manifest in various ways, and its signs are not always immediately obvious. Partners may hide their pain due to fear, shame, or the desire to appear strong. Recognizing trauma involves being observant and sensitive to subtle changes in behavior, mood, and physical health. Here are some key signs and indicators to watch for:

Emotional Indicators

- *Mood Swings:* Sudden and intense changes in mood can be a sign of unresolved trauma. Your partner might experience rapid shifts from happiness to sadness, anger, or anxiety without a clear trigger.

- *Persistent Sadness or Depression:* If your partner frequently feels hopeless, helpless, or profoundly sad, it could indicate underlying trauma. Depression may manifest as a loss of interest in activities they once enjoyed, changes in appetite or sleep patterns, and general lethargy.

- *Anxiety and Fear:* Trauma often leaves individuals in a constant state of high alert. Your partner may seem excessively worried or fearful about everyday situations, avoiding places or activities that remind them of their traumatic experiences.

- *Anger and Irritability:* Anger can be a defence mechanism to mask deeper feelings of hurt and vulnerability. If your partner displays frequent irritability or disproportionate anger, it may stem from unresolved trauma.

Psychological Indicators

1. *Intrusive Thoughts and Flashbacks:* Your partner may experience recurring, distressing memories of the traumatic event. Flashbacks can be so vivid that they feel as though they are reliving the trauma, often triggered by certain sounds, smells, or sights.
2. *Difficulty Concentrating:* Trauma can impair cognitive functions, making it hard for your partner to focus or remember things. They might seem forgetful, easily distracted, or struggle with decision-making.
3. *Dissociation:* Some trauma survivors cope by mentally

distancing themselves from the present moment. This can manifest as a sense of detachment, feeling numb, or as if they are observing themselves from outside their body.

Behavioral Indicators

- *Avoidance Behaviors:* Your partner may go to great lengths to avoid people, places, or activities that remind them of the trauma. This can lead to isolation, withdrawal from social interactions, and a narrowing of their world.

- *Changes in Social Interaction:* Noticeable changes in how your partner interacts with others can be a sign of trauma. They may become more withdrawn, have difficulty trusting others, or seem overly dependent on certain individuals.

- *Substance Abuse:* Using alcohol or drugs to cope with emotional pain is common among trauma survivors. If your partner's substance use has increased or seems out of control, it might be a coping mechanism for dealing with trauma.

- *Self-Destructive Behaviors:* Engaging in risky or self-harming behaviors, such as reckless driving, unprotected sex, or self-mutilation, can be a way for trauma survivors to express their pain or attempt to regain control over their lives.

Physical Indicators

- *Chronic Pain and Health Issues:* Trauma can manifest as chronic physical pain, often with no apparent medical cause. Your partner may frequently complain of headaches, stomach aches, or other unexplained ailments.

- *Sleep Disturbances:* Difficulty falling or staying asleep, frequent nightmares, and restless sleep are common among trauma survivors. Pay attention if your partner's sleep patterns have significantly changed.

- *Changes in Appearance:* Trauma can affect self-care routines. Your partner might neglect their personal hygiene, dress differently, or experience significant weight changes due to altered eating habits.

Common Behaviors

Understanding the behaviors associated with trauma helps in identifying and addressing them compassionately. Here are some common behaviors that may stem from trauma:

Withdrawal and Isolation: Many trauma survivors withdraw from social interactions as a protective mechanism. They might avoid gatherings, stop participating in activities they once enjoyed, or isolate themselves even from close friends and family. This withdrawal can be driven by a fear of judgment, a desire to avoid triggering situations, or a belief that others cannot understand their pain.

- *Emotional Withdrawal:* Beyond physical isolation, your partner might also withdraw emotionally. They may seem distant, unresponsive, or uninterested in engaging in meaningful conversations.
- *Social Avoidance:* Your partner might avoid places or activities that remind them of the trauma, leading to a decline in social engagements and interactions.

Anger and Irritability: Trauma can cause significant emotional turmoil, which often manifests as anger and irritability. These outbursts may seem disproportionate to the situation and can be directed at both loved ones and strangers.

- *Frequent Arguments:* Your partner might engage in more frequent arguments, sometimes over trivial matters. This can be a way of expressing their inner turmoil or attempting to regain a sense of control.

- *Short Temper:* A shorter temper or quicker to frustration than usual can be a sign of underlying distress. They might react aggressively to perceived slights or challenges.

Hypervigilance and Anxiety: Hypervigilance is a state of heightened alertness where your partner is constantly on the lookout for potential threats. This can lead to excessive worry, difficulty relaxing, and a pervasive sense of anxiety.

- *Constant Scanning:* Your partner may constantly scan their environment for potential dangers, even in safe settings. This can make them seem distracted or on edge.
- *Excessive Worrying:* They might worry excessively about future events or potential risks, often imagining worst-case scenarios.

Avoidance and Numbing: Avoidance behaviors are common in trauma survivors as they try to steer clear of anything that might trigger painful memories. Numbing, on the other hand, is an emotional defense mechanism where individuals shut down their feelings to avoid distress.

- *Avoiding Conversations:* Your partner might avoid talking about the trauma or anything related to it, changing the subject or becoming visibly uncomfortable when it comes up.
- *Emotional Numbing:* They may appear detached or unresponsive, struggling to experience positive emotions or feeling disconnected from their own feelings and those of others.

Self-Destructive Behaviors: Engaging in self-destructive behaviors can be a way for trauma survivors to cope with their pain or attempt to regain a sense of control over their lives.

- *Substance Abuse:* Increased use of alcohol or drugs to numb emotional pain is a typical response to trauma.
- *Risk-Taking:* Reckless behaviors, such as dangerous driving, unprotected sex, or physical altercations, can be ways to externalize internal chaos or seek a sense of control.

Dissociation: Dissociation involves a sense of detachment from reality, which can manifest in various ways. Your partner might seem spaced out, lost in thought, or as if they are not fully present.

- *Daydreaming or Zoning Out: Your partner might frequently zone out or seem disconnected from their surroundings* as if they are lost in their thoughts.
- *Memory Gaps:* They may have trouble remembering certain events or details, particularly those related to the trauma.

Recognizing trauma in your partner involves observing their emotional, psychological, behavioral, and physical responses to various situations. Understanding these signs and behaviors is the first step in providing the necessary support and fostering a compassionate, understanding relationship. It is crucial to approach these signs with empathy, avoiding judgment or assumptions, and to create a safe space for your partner to express their feelings and experiences. By recognizing and understanding the signs of trauma, you can begin to support your partner in their healing journey.

In the next chapters, we will explore strategies for effective communication, building trust, and creating a safe environment, all essential components for navigating a relationship affected by trauma. Together, you can work towards healing and building a relationship that is resilient, loving, and supportive.

CHAPTER THREE
Communication & Empathy

Effective communication and empathy are essential components of every successful relationship, particularly when one partner has suffered trauma. This chapter discusses the value of open communication and offers ways to empathize with your partner's experiences, resulting in a stronger connection and mutual understanding.

Open and honest communication is vital in a relationship where trauma is present. It allows both partners to express their feelings, share their experiences, and work through challenges together. Transparent communication builds trust, reduces misunderstandings, and creates a supportive environment for healing.

Creating a safe space for communication means establishing an environment where both partners feel comfortable sharing their thoughts and feelings without fear of judgment or reprisal. This involves active listening, validating emotions, and maintaining a non-judgmental attitude.

- *Active Listening:* Practice active listening by giving your full attention to your partner when they speak. Show that you are engaged by nodding, maintaining eye contact, and providing verbal affirmations like "I understand" or "I'm here for you." Avoid interrupting or offering unsolicited advice; sometimes, your partner needs to be heard.

- *Validating Emotions:* Acknowledge your partner's emotions and experiences and validate them. Use phrases like "It's understandable that you feel this way" or "I can see why that would be upsetting." Validation helps your partner feel seen and heard, fostering a sense of security and trust.

- *Non-Judgmental Attitude:* Approach conversations with an open mind, avoiding judgments or assumptions about your partner's experiences or reactions. Remember that their feelings and responses are valid, even if they differ from your own perspective.

Encouraging Open Dialogue: Encouraging open dialogue involves creating opportunities for meaningful conversations about past experiences and current challenges. This can be challenging, as discussing trauma is often painful and requires vulnerability.

- *Asking Open-Ended Questions:* Use open-ended questions to encourage your partner to share their thoughts and feelings. Questions like "How are you feeling today?" or "Can you tell me more about that experience?" invite your partner to open up without feeling pressured.

- *Setting Aside Time for Conversations:* Set aside regular times to talk, ensuring that you both have the space and time to engage in deep, uninterrupted conversations. This shows your commitment to understanding and supporting your partner.

- *Respecting Boundaries:* While it's important to encourage open dialogue, it's equally crucial to respect your partner's boundaries. If they are not ready to talk about certain topics, don't push them. Let them know that you are there for them whenever they are ready to share.

Navigating Difficult Conversations: Difficult conversations are inevitable when dealing with trauma. Learning how to navigate these conversations with sensitivity and care is essential for maintaining a supportive relationship.

- *Staying Calm and Patient:* Remain calm and patient during difficult conversations, even if emotions run high. Your partner may express anger, frustration, or sadness, and it's important to respond with empathy and understanding rather than defensiveness or anger.

- *Using "I" Statements:* When discussing sensitive topics, use "I" statements to express your feelings and needs without blaming or criticizing your partner. For example, say "I feel worried when you withdraw because I care about you" instead of "You always shut me out."

- *Seeking Professional Help:* If conversations become too challenging to manage on your own, consider seeking the help of a therapist or counselor. Professional guidance can provide both partners with the tools and support needed to navigate difficult conversations and work through trauma.

Empathy and Understanding

Empathy is the ability to understand and share another person's feelings. In a relationship where trauma is present, empathy involves recognizing the impact of your partner's experiences and responding with compassion and support. Developing empathy requires active effort and a willingness to learn and grow together.

Understanding the Nature of Trauma

To empathize with your partner, it's important to understand the nature of trauma and its effects. Educate yourself about the different types of trauma, the common symptoms and behaviors, and the long-term impact it can have on an individual's life.

- *Educating Yourself:* Read books, articles, and research studies on trauma to gain a deeper understanding of its complexities. Attending workshops or support groups can also provide valuable insights and perspectives.
- *Learning from Your Partner:* Your partner is the best source of information about their own experiences. Listen to their stories, ask questions, and show genuine interest in understanding their unique journey.

Practicing Empathy in Everyday Interactions

Practicing empathy in everyday interactions is about putting yourself in your partner's shoes and responding with kindness and understanding. This can be particularly challenging when your partner's behavior is difficult to understand or manage. One important aspect of empathy is showing compassion, which involves recognizing your partner's pain and offering support and comfort. Simple gestures like holding their hand, offering a hug, or saying "I'm here for you" can make a significant difference in how they feel. Being patient is another critical component, as healing from trauma is a long and often unpredictable process. It's essential to be patient with your partner and understand that progress may be slow and setbacks are normal. Avoid putting pressure on them to "get over" their trauma or expecting them to heal on your timeline. I would also like to point out that offering support is also crucial. This can be done in practical ways, such as helping with daily tasks, attending therapy sessions together, or finding resources for healing. Showing that you are committed to their well-being and willing to walk this journey with them can reinforce your support and strengthen your relationship.

Building Emotional Resilience Together
Building emotional resilience together involves developing the skills and resources needed to cope with stress and adversity. By building resilience together, you can strengthen your relationship and support each other through difficult times. A key aspect of this is developing coping strategies. Work together to find healthy ways to manage stress and trauma-related symptoms, such as mindfulness practices, physical exercise, creative activities, or relaxation techniques. Another important component is creating a support network. Surround yourselves with supportive friends, family, and professionals who can provide additional help and encouragement. A strong support network can alleviate some of the pressure on your relationship and offer a broader base of support. Additionally, fostering positive experiences is crucial. Focus on creating moments of joy, laughter, and connection to counterbalance the challenges of dealing with trauma. Engaging in activities that bring happiness can help build positive memories and strengthen your bond, making it easier to navigate difficult times together.

Celebrating Progress and Milestones
Celebrating progress and milestones, no matter how small, is essential for maintaining motivation and a sense of hope. It's important to acknowledge and appreciate the efforts your partner is making and to celebrate your achievements together. Recognizing small victories is a crucial part of this process. Celebrate the little wins, like a day without anxiety, a successful therapy session, or a positive social interaction. These moments are important steps in the healing journey and deserve recognition. Additionally, setting realistic goals for your relationship and your partner's healing process can provide clear milestones to aim for. When you reach these goals, celebrate them to reinforce the progress and effort made. Expressing gratitude regularly for each other and the efforts you both put in is also vital. By acknowledging and appreciating each other's contributions, you create a positive and supportive environment that strengthens your bond and helps you both stay motivated on the path to healing.

Effective communication and empathy are essential components of a trauma-informed partnership. Partners may cultivate open communication, provide a safe environment for discourse, and practice empathy to develop a supportive and understanding partnership. It is a journey that needs patience, kindness, and a willingness to learn and develop together.

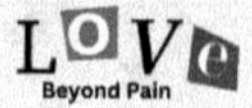

CHAPTER FOUR

Building Trust & Safety

Any healthy relationship must be built on trust and safety, but dealing with trauma requires these two elements more than ever. Trauma can severely disrupt a person's sense of safety and trust, making it crucial for their partner to help restore these foundations. This chapter focuses on creating a secure atmosphere and taking deliberate actions to rebuild trust that may have been affected by trauma-related behaviors.

The first step in supporting your partner is to create a safe environment. This involves addressing both physical and emotional aspects to foster a nurturing and protective space. On the physical side, safety entails creating a stable and predictable environment. Trauma can make the world seem chaotic, so establishing a routine can provide a sense of stability. Consistent daily activities, regular meal times, and a reliable sleep schedule can help make your surroundings more predictable. Additionally, designating a specific area of your home as a "safe space" where your partner can retreat when feeling overwhelmed is essential. This space should be comfortable, quiet, and free from stressors. Personalizing it with comforting items like favorite books, blankets, or music can enhance the feeling of safety. It's also important to respect your partner's physical boundaries. Trauma survivors may be more sensitive to physical touch or proximity, so always ask for consent before initiating contact and be attentive to their non-verbal cues.

Emotional safety is equally important. It involves creating an environment where your partner feels emotionally secure and supported. Maintaining a non-judgmental attitude is crucial; approach all interactions with acceptance and avoid criticizing or blaming your partner for their feelings or reactions, even if they seem irrational. Practicing active listening—where you give your full attention and empathy—is another key element. Show that you value their experiences and emotions by validating their feelings. Being consistent and reliable builds emotional safety by reinforcing trust and demonstrating your commitment to their well-being. Consistently following through on your promises helps rebuild trust. Encouraging open communication is also vital. Foster an environment where your partner feels safe to express their thoughts and feelings without fear of judgment or rejection.

Creating a trauma-informed environment involves understanding the unique needs and triggers of trauma survivors. Start by working with your partner to identify specific triggers—things that may cause distress or anxiety, such as certain sounds, smells, places, or situations that remind them of their trauma. Once identified, take steps to minimize these triggers in your environment. This might involve altering routines, avoiding certain places, or making adjustments to your home. Additionally, help your partner develop coping strategies for dealing with unavoidable triggers. This could include deep breathing exercises, mindfulness practices, or having a plan for managing distressing situations. By addressing these elements, you can help create a supportive environment that facilitates healing and strengthens your relationship.

Rebuilding Trust

Rebuilding trust after trauma can be a gradual and challenging process, as trauma deeply affects an individual's ability to trust others. It is essential to approach this process with deliberate and thoughtful steps. Honesty and transparency play a crucial role in rebuilding trust. Being open about your intentions, actions, and feelings creates a foundation of trustworthiness. This means communicating honestly with your partner, even about difficult topics, as avoiding or sugar-coating the truth can lead to misunderstandings and erode trust. Acknowledging and apologizing for mistakes is also vital, as taking responsibility demonstrates integrity and a commitment to the relationship. Transparency involves sharing relevant information and being open about your thoughts and feelings, which helps to build a sense of security and predictability in the relationship.

Consistency and reliability are essential components in this rebuilding process. Being a consistent and reliable partner helps establish a sense of security and dependability. This involves following through on promises and commitments, whether small or significant. Honoring your word builds trust and reliability. Additionally, being predictable in your actions and behavior creates a stable environment that provides a sense of stability for your partner. Regularly spending time together and being

available during times of need further reinforces your reliability and commitment.

Rebuilding trust also requires patience and understanding. It is important to recognize that the process takes time, and setbacks are a natural part of healing. Being patient with your partner is crucial, as rushing them to "move on" or "get over" their trauma can be counterproductive. Demonstrating empathy by putting yourself in your partner's shoes and understanding their feelings and experiences helps build a deeper connection and fosters trust. Supporting their healing process actively by encouraging professional help, therapeutic activities, and self-care practices is also important.

Creating positive experiences together can help build new, positive memories that counterbalance the negative impact of trauma. Engaging in shared activities that both partners enjoy fosters a sense of connection, while celebrating achievements and milestones, no matter how small, reinforces a sense of accomplishment and builds positive memories. Establishing new traditions and rituals that bring joy and a sense of belonging can also provide comfort and stability in the relationship.

Seeking professional help can be beneficial in this process. Couples therapy can assist both partners in navigating the challenges of rebuilding trust and improving communication, offering strategies for fostering trust and addressing trauma-related issues. Individual therapy can support your partner in working through their trauma, providing a safe space for them to process their experiences and develop coping strategies. Support groups for trauma survivors can offer additional support and a sense of community, which can be beneficial for healing.

Rebuilding trust and establishing safety in a relationship affected by trauma requires conscious effort, persistence, and compassion. Partners can cultivate a loving and supportive connection by creating a safe atmosphere, working to reestablish trust, understanding the specific needs of trauma survivors, and maintaining a consistent and supportive presence.

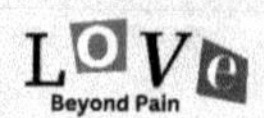
LOVe
Beyond Pain

CHAPTER FIVE

Supporting Your Partners Healing Journey

Encouraging Professional Help

Helping a partner through their trauma-related healing process is a meaningful but challenging commitment. It requires sensitivity, patience, understanding, and a readiness to navigate both the highs and lows of their recovery journey. This chapter highlights the importance of seeking professional therapy and offers practical advice for being a supportive spouse throughout the recovery process.

Encouraging your partner to seek professional help is crucial, as therapy and counseling provide the necessary tools and support for managing trauma and starting the path to recovery. Therapy offers a structured, safe environment where trauma survivors can explore their experiences, process emotions, and develop coping strategies. It provides a confidential and non-judgmental space where your partner can openly discuss their trauma without fear of judgment. This space is vital for addressing difficult emotions and experiences.

Professional therapists are trained to handle the complex nature of trauma, helping individuals identify and address the root causes of their pain. By understanding the origins of their trauma, your partner can begin to heal. Therapists also teach effective coping strategies to manage trauma-related symptoms, which can help your partner navigate daily life with greater resilience. Beyond immediate relief, therapy focuses on long-term healing and personal growth, enabling your partner to gain a deeper understanding of themselves and their trauma, leading to sustained recovery and well-being.

Encouraging your partner to seek help should be done with sensitivity and respect for their feelings and autonomy. Normalize the idea of therapy by discussing its benefits openly and without stigma. Share positive stories of others who have benefited from therapy, emphasizing that seeking help is a common and effective step towards healing. Express your concern with compassion, using "I" statements to convey your feelings, such as "I care about you and want to see you feel better" or "I believe therapy could help you manage what you're going through." Offer practical information about therapy options, including different types of therapy, potential therapists, and how to access services, to make the process less daunting. Respect their autonomy in making the decision to seek therapy, and support their choice, whatever it may be.

Finding the right therapist is a crucial step in the healing process. It's important that the therapist's approach, personality, and expertise align with your partner's needs. Research potential therapists who specialize in trauma and have positive reviews and relevant credentials. Encourage your partner to consider their comfort and fit with potential therapists, as the therapeutic relationship should feel safe and supportive. If the first therapist they try isn't the right fit, encourage them to keep searching until they find someone who feels right. Additionally, there are various types of therapy that can be effective for trauma, such as Cognitive Behavioral Therapy (CBT), Eye Movement Desensitization and Reprocessing (EMDR), and somatic therapies. Encourage your partner to explore different modalities to find what works best for them.

Supporting your partner through their trauma recovery involves understanding the importance of professional help, encouraging them with empathy, and assisting them in finding the right resources. By fostering a supportive environment and respecting their journey, you can help them on the path to healing and recovery.

Being A Supportive Partner

Being a supportive partner through your loved one's trauma recovery involves offering emotional, practical, and consistent support. Your role is to be a steady, understanding presence that reinforces their efforts to heal and grow.

Emotional support is fundamental in this process. This means being present and empathetic, and validating their experiences and feelings. Practice active listening by showing empathy and understanding without jumping in with unsolicited advice or judgment. Allow your partner the space to express their emotions and experiences freely. Validation can be as simple as acknowledging their feelings with statements like, "I can see how that would be really hard for you" or "Your feelings are completely valid." It's also crucial to be patient and compassionate, understanding that healing from trauma is a long and often non-linear journey. Recognize that progress may be slow and setbacks are part of the process. Avoid expressing frustration or impatience as this can hinder their healing.

Practical support is another important aspect. This involves helping with everyday tasks and responsibilities to ease their burden as they focus on their recovery. Offer assistance with daily activities such as cooking, cleaning, or running errands. Supporting their self-care practices is also vital; help them establish a self-care routine, join them in physical activities, or remind them to take time for themselves. If they are comfortable, accompany them to therapy or medical appointments to provide additional support and reassurance.

Maintaining consistency and reliability is key to building trust and providing a stable support system. Show up consistently and be a dependable presence in their life. Follow through on your commitments and be there when you say you will be. Help create and maintain a routine that offers a sense of stability and predictability, which can be particularly comforting for trauma survivors who may feel a lack of control. Regularly reassure your partner of your support and commitment with affirmations like, "I'm here for you" or "We'll get through this together."

While providing support, it's also important to respect and encourage your partner's independence and autonomy. Empower them to make their own decisions and take ownership of their healing process. Support them in setting their own goals and determining the steps they need to take. Balance offering support with fostering independence; assist when needed but also encourage them to engage in self-care practices on their own. Recognize and celebrate their strengths and achievements, no matter how small, and acknowledge their resilience and progress.

Supporting your partner through their healing journey after trauma is a profound act of love and commitment. By encouraging professional help and being a supportive partner, you play a crucial role in their recovery. This journey demands empathy, patience, and a deep understanding of the complexities of trauma and healing.

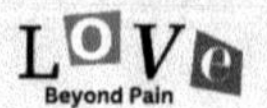

CHAPTER SIX

Coping with Challenging Behaviors

Understanding Trauma Responses

Trauma can lead to a variety of challenging behaviors that may strain relationships. Understanding why these behaviors occur and learning how to respond can help partners navigate these difficulties more effectively. Trauma responses are often rooted in deep-seated fear and the body's attempt to protect itself from further harm. These responses can manifest in various ways, including emotional outbursts, withdrawal, and hypervigilance. Understanding the origins of these behaviors can help partners respond with empathy and support. Trauma survivors may exhibit one or more of the four primary trauma responses: flight, fight, freeze, and fawn. Each response is a survival mechanism that the body uses to cope with perceived threats. The flight response involves the urge to escape or avoid situations that trigger trauma memories, which can manifest as physical avoidance, excessive

busyness, or distancing oneself from relationships and responsibilities. The fight response is characterized by aggression or defensiveness, including angry outbursts, irritability, or confrontational behavior, often as a way to regain control and protect oneself from perceived threats. The freeze response involves a sense of paralysis or inability to act, manifesting as dissociation, numbness, or a feeling of being stuck, often as a way to cope with overwhelming emotions. The fawn response involves people-pleasing or submissive behavior to avoid conflict and secure safety, including excessive compliance, difficulty saying no, or prioritizing others' needs over one's own.

Understanding the common behaviors associated with trauma responses can help partners identify the underlying causes and respond appropriately. Trauma survivors may withdraw from social interactions and isolate themselves to avoid triggers and potential harm, a behavior often stemming from a fear of being overwhelmed or retraumatized. Anger and irritability can be manifestations of the fight response, as the survivor attempts to regain control and protect themselves, triggered by feelings of helplessness or perceived threats. Hypervigilance involves being constantly on alert for potential danger, often resulting from the body's heightened stress response, leading to chronic anxiety and difficulty relaxing. Trauma can severely impact a person's ability to trust others, manifesting as suspicion, reluctance to share personal information, or difficulty forming close relationships.

Responding to trauma responses with empathy and understanding can help de-escalate situations and provide a supportive environment for healing. When your partner exhibits challenging behaviors, strive to remain calm and patient, avoiding reacting with anger or frustration, as this can exacerbate the situation. Acknowledge and validate your partner's feelings, even if you don't fully understand them, letting them know that their emotions are valid and that you are there to support them. Provide reassurance and comfort during moments of distress, with simple affirmations such as "I'm here for you" or "You're safe with me" helping to calm their anxiety and reinforce a sense of security. Encourage your partner to engage in healthy coping mechanisms, such as mindfulness practices, exercise, or creative outlets, which can help them manage their emotions and reduce stress.

Understanding trauma responses and responding with empathy are crucial steps in navigating the challenging behaviors that can arise from trauma. By maintaining a calm and supportive presence, partners can help create an environment conducive to healing and growth. Recognizing and validating the survivor's feelings, providing consistent reassurance, and encouraging healthy coping strategies can significantly impact their journey toward recovery.

Setting Boundaries

Setting healthy boundaries is essential for both partners in a relationship affected by trauma. Boundaries help to create a safe and respectful environment, prevent burnout, and ensure that both partners' needs are met. They are vital for maintaining emotional health and relationship stability, defining personal limits, and ensuring that both partners feel respected and valued. Boundaries protect your emotional well-being by preventing you from becoming overwhelmed or resentful, helping you maintain a sense of self, and ensuring that your needs are not neglected.

They foster mutual respect by clearly defining acceptable behavior and expectations, creating a balanced relationship where both partners' needs and boundaries are honored. Supporting a partner through trauma can be emotionally taxing, and setting boundaries helps to prevent burnout by ensuring that you have the time and space to recharge and care for yourself.

Identifying your personal boundaries is the first step in establishing and maintaining them within your relationship. Reflecting on your needs is crucial; take time to consider what behaviors or situations make you feel uncomfortable, stressed, or overwhelmed. Communicating boundaries clearly and assertively to your partner using "I" statements, such as "I need time alone to recharge" or "I feel uncomfortable when you raise your voice," ensures that your needs are understood. Revisiting boundaries regularly is important as they may need to be adjusted over time as both partners grow and change, ensuring they continue to meet your needs.

Respecting your partner's boundaries is equally important for maintaining a healthy relationship. Listening to your partner's boundaries without judgment or defensiveness, acknowledging their needs, and showing respect for their limits is vital. Avoiding boundary violations, such as respecting their need for alone time, not pushing them to discuss their trauma, and avoiding triggering situations, helps maintain trust. Encouraging open communication about boundaries and being willing to discuss and adjust them as needed fosters a supportive and understanding relationship.

Creating joint boundaries as a couple can help to strengthen your relationship and provide a unified approach to handling challenges. Discussing shared values and goals as a couple can help identify areas where joint boundaries are needed to support your relationship. Setting relationship rules that align with your shared values and goals, such as guidelines for communication, conflict resolution, and personal space, helps maintain harmony. Supporting each other's growth ensures that your joint boundaries encourage mutual support and allow both partners to thrive individually and as a couple.

Understanding, sensitivity, and clear limits are required to cope with problematic behaviors in a traumatized relationship. Partners may establish a supportive atmosphere that promotes recovery by detecting trauma responses and reacting compassionately. Setting and respecting appropriate boundaries ensures that both partners' needs are satisfied while maintaining the relationship's balance and respect.

CHAPTER SEVEN

Self-Care for the Supporting Partner

Providing trauma support to a spouse can be emotionally taxing and difficult. It is critical for the supportive spouse to prioritize self-care in order to preserve their own health and continue offering good assistance. This chapter highlights the significance of self-care and suggests ways for finding support networks to help the supportive partner.

Maintaining Your Own Well-being

Self-care is not selfish; it's essential for the well-being of both partners in a relationship affected by trauma. Taking care of yourself enables you to remain emotionally resilient, supportive, and compassionate toward your partner.

Stress the Importance of Self-Care

Self-care involves deliberate actions that promote physical, emotional, and mental well-being. It is a proactive approach to managing stress, preventing burnout, and maintaining overall health.

- *Physical Self-Care:* Prioritize physical health by engaging in regular exercise, maintaining a balanced diet, and getting enough sleep. Physical well-being supports emotional resilience and provides energy to cope with daily challenges.

- *Emotional Self-Care:* Pay attention to your emotional needs and practice techniques that promote emotional well-being. This may include journaling, practicing mindfulness or meditation, and expressing your feelings through creative outlets.

- *Mental Self-Care:* Protect your mental health by engaging in activities that stimulate your mind and promote relaxation. This could involve reading, learning new skills, or engaging in hobbies that bring you joy and fulfillment.

Setting Boundaries for Self-Care

Establishing boundaries is crucial for protecting your own well-being while supporting your partner through their healing journey.

- *Balancing Support and Independence:* Strive to maintain a balance between supporting your partner and attending to your own needs. Recognize when you need time alone or additional support from others.

- *Communicating Your Needs:* Clearly communicate your self-care needs to your partner. Express the importance of taking breaks and engaging in activities that recharge you, without guilt or resentment.

- *Prioritizing Time for Yourself:* Schedule regular periods of self-care into your routine. This may include designated "me time" for relaxation, hobbies, or activities that bring you pleasure and rejuvenation.

Seeking Support

Support networks provide a valuable source of guidance, understanding, and emotional sustenance for the supporting partner. Seeking support from others reinforces your own resilience and ability to provide effective support to your partner.

Encouraging Support Networks

Building a support network involves connecting with trusted individuals who can offer empathy, advice, and encouragement during challenging times.

- *Friends and Family:* Lean on friends and family members who are understanding and supportive. Share your experiences and feelings with trusted loved ones who can provide a listening ear and emotional support.
- *Support Groups:* Consider joining support groups for partners of trauma survivors or caregivers. These groups offer a sense of community, shared experiences, and practical strategies for coping with the challenges of supporting a loved one through trauma.
- *Professional Support:* Seek guidance from mental health professionals, such as therapists or counselors, who specialize in supporting caregivers or partners of trauma survivors. Professional support can offer valuable insights and coping strategies tailored to your specific needs.

Practicing Self-Compassion

Self-compassion involves treating yourself with the same kindness and understanding that you would offer to others facing similar challenges.

- *Acknowledging Your Efforts:* Recognize and celebrate your efforts in supporting your partner through trauma. Acknowledge the emotional strength and resilience that you demonstrate on a daily basis.

- *Forgiving Yourself:* Let go of self-criticism and perfectionism. Understand that it's normal to feel overwhelmed or uncertain at times. Forgive yourself for mistakes and focus on learning and growth.

- *Being Kind to Yourself:* Practice self-care rituals that promote self-compassion, such as positive self-talk, self-affirmations, and engaging in activities that bring you joy and fulfillment.

Setting Realistic Expectations

Setting realistic expectations for yourself as a supporting partner is essential for maintaining emotional well-being and preventing burnout.

- *Accepting Limitations:* Recognize that you cannot fix or heal your partner's trauma on your own. Accept that healing is a gradual process that requires patience, time, and professional support.

- *Understanding Your Role:* Clarify your role as a supportive partner. Focus on offering empathy, validation, and practical assistance, while encouraging your partner to seek professional help and engage in self-care practices.

- *Celebrating Small Victories:* Celebrate small victories and progress in your partner's healing journey. Acknowledge the positive impact of your support and the resilience that you both demonstrate throughout the process.

Self-care is not only good but also necessary for the supportive spouse in a traumatized relationship. Prioritizing your own well-being and accessing support networks can allow you to maintain your emotional resilience while also offering appropriate assistance to your spouse.

Remember that taking care of yourself allows you to better care for others and handle the hurdles of accompanying a loved one on their healing path.

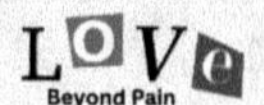

CHAPTER EIGHT

Navigating Relationship Dynamics

Navigating interpersonal dynamics in the aftermath of trauma needs empathy, tolerance, and a dedication to creating a healthy and supportive atmosphere. This chapter focuses on healthy relationship practices and conflict resolution solutions for trauma-related difficulties.

Healthy Relationship Practices

Maintaining a healthy relationship is essential for supporting each other's well-being and fostering growth and intimacy. Implementing healthy relationship practices promotes mutual respect, communication, and trust.

Tips for Maintaining a Healthy Relationship

Healthy relationships are built on a foundation of trust, open communication, and mutual support. Consider these tips for nurturing a strong and resilient relationship:

- *Communication:* Foster open and honest communication with your partner. Practice active listening, empathy, and validation to strengthen emotional intimacy and understanding.

- *Trust:* Build and maintain trust through consistency, reliability, and honesty. Trust is essential for feeling secure and supported in the relationship.

- *Respect:* Show respect for each other's thoughts, feelings, and boundaries. Respectful behavior fosters a sense of equality and appreciation within the relationship.

- *Support:* Offer emotional, practical, and moral support to each other. Supportive behaviors demonstrate commitment and solidarity during challenging times.

- *Quality Time:* Prioritize quality time together to nurture connection and intimacy. Engage in shared activities, meaningful conversations, and moments of relaxation.

- *Personal Growth:* Encourage and support each other's personal growth and development. Celebrate achievements and navigate challenges together as a team.

Cultivating Emotional Intimacy

Emotional intimacy involves sharing vulnerabilities, feelings, and experiences with your partner in a safe and trusting environment.

- *Vulnerability:* Share your thoughts, emotions, and fears with your partner. Vulnerability fosters closeness and strengthens emotional bonds.

- *Empathy:* Practice empathy by understanding and validating your partner's experiences and emotions. Empathetic responses promote mutual understanding and connection.

- *Affection:* Show affection through physical touch, verbal affirmations, and acts of kindness. Affection reinforces feelings of love, appreciation, and security in the relationship.

- *Conflict Resolution:* Address conflicts promptly and constructively. Approach disagreements with patience, respect, and a willingness to compromise.

Conflict Resolution

Conflict is a natural part of any relationship, and navigating conflicts related to trauma requires sensitivity, patience, and effective communication strategies.

Strategies for Resolving Conflicts

Conflict resolution is crucial for maintaining harmony and mutual understanding in a relationship affected by trauma-related issues.

- *Active Listening:* Listen actively and attentively to your partner's concerns and perspectives. Validate their feelings and demonstrate empathy before expressing your own viewpoint.

- *Expressing Feelings:* Use "I" statements to express your feelings and experiences without blaming or accusing your partner. For example, "I feel hurt when..." or "I would like..."

- *Seeking Understanding:* Seek to understand your partner's underlying emotions and needs. Ask clarifying questions and paraphrase their concerns to ensure mutual understanding.

- *Finding Common Ground:* Identify common goals and interests to guide the resolution process. Focus on collaborative solutions that prioritize the well-being and happiness of both partners.

- *Compromise and Flexibility:* Be willing to compromise and find middle ground when addressing conflicting needs or preferences. Flexibility allows for adjustments and adaptations as the relationship evolves.

- *Taking Breaks:* If tensions escalate, take a break to cool off and regain perspective. Agree on a time to revisit the discussion with a calm and clear mindset.

- *Seeking Mediation:* Consider seeking mediation or couples therapy to facilitate constructive communication and conflict resolution. A neutral third party can provide guidance and support in navigating sensitive issues.

Handling interpersonal dynamics in the aftermath of trauma needs deliberate work, sensitivity, and a dedication to cultivating a healthy and supportive partnership. Healthy relationship practices and conflict resolution skills may help couples improve their emotional connection, create trust, and negotiate obstacles with resilience and compassion.

CHAPTER NINE

Hope and Moving Forward

As partners traverse the intricacies of helping one other through trauma, fostering hope and resilience becomes critical to maintaining a positive and forward-thinking outlook. This chapter discusses the significance of recognizing progress, having an optimistic mindset, and embracing optimism as couples move forward in their healing journey.

Celebrating Progress

Celebrating progress acknowledges the resilience and growth achieved by both partners throughout the healing process. Recognizing milestones encourages positivity and reinforces the commitment to supporting each other's well-being.

Recognizing Healing Milestones

Healing from trauma is a gradual process marked by significant milestones and achievements. Celebrate these moments to acknowledge progress and reinforce resilience:

- *Personal Growth:* Reflect on the personal growth and development achieved by each partner. Celebrate moments of strength, courage, and perseverance.

- *Relationship Milestones:* Recognize milestones in your relationship, such as moments of connection, intimacy, and mutual understanding. Celebrate achievements in communication, conflict resolution, and mutual support.

- *Healing Milestones:* Acknowledge milestones in your partner's healing journey, such as breakthroughs in therapy, increased self-awareness, and coping with triggers. Celebrate moments of healing and resilience.

Expressing Gratitude and Appreciation

Express gratitude and appreciation for each other's efforts and support throughout the healing process. Gratitude fosters positivity and strengthens emotional bonds:

- *Verbal Affirmations:* Share heartfelt compliments and expressions of gratitude. Acknowledge the strengths and qualities that inspire admiration and appreciation.

- *Acts of Kindness:* Show appreciation through thoughtful gestures and acts of kindness. Small gestures, such as helping with chores or preparing a favorite meal, demonstrate care and support.

Creating Rituals of Celebration

Establish rituals or traditions to commemorate milestones and achievements. Rituals provide a sense of continuity, connection, and shared meaning within the relationship:

- *Celebratory Dinners or Activities:* Plan special dinners, outings, or activities to celebrate milestones together. Choose activities that hold personal significance and promote enjoyment and relaxation.

- *Journaling and Reflection:* Keep a shared journal or scrapbook to document milestones, reflections, and expressions of gratitude. Reviewing these memories reinforces the journey of healing and growth.

- *Shared Goals and Aspirations:* Set and celebrate shared goals and aspirations for the future. Celebrate progress toward these goals as a testament to your partnership's strength and resilience.

Maintaining a Positive Outlook

Maintaining a positive outlook is crucial for navigating challenges and fostering hope within the relationship. Embrace optimism and resilience as partners continue to support each other through ups and downs:

Embracing Optimism

Optimism involves focusing on possibilities, strengths, and opportunities for growth despite challenges. Embrace optimism as a guiding principle in your relationship:

- *Focus on Strengths:* Identify and nurture each other's strengths and positive qualities. Recognize resilience, determination, and adaptability in overcoming obstacles.

- *Gratitude Practice:* Cultivate a daily gratitude practice to foster positivity and perspective. Reflect on blessings, moments of joy, and sources of strength within your relationship.

- Positive Affirmations: Repeat positive affirmations and beliefs about your relationship's resilience and ability to overcome challenges. Affirmations reinforce a mindset of hope and possibility.

Building Resilience

Resilience is the ability to bounce back from adversity and continue moving forward. Strengthen resilience within your relationship through adaptive coping strategies:

- *Flexibility and Adaptability:* Embrace flexibility and adaptability when navigating unexpected challenges or setbacks. Approach obstacles as opportunities for growth and learning.

- *Problem-Solving Skills:* Enhance problem-solving skills by collaboratively addressing challenges and finding creative solutions. Focus on constructive communication and mutual support.

- *Self-Care and Well-being:* Prioritize self-care practices that promote physical, emotional, and mental well-being. Nurturing your own resilience supports your ability to support your partner.

In traumatized relationships, hope may be a powerful driver for healing and progress. Partners who celebrate progress, maintain a positive perspective, and embrace resilience may traverse the complexity of trauma with hope and persistence. Each milestone and success builds on the relationship's foundation of trust, love, and mutual support.

LOVe
Beyond Pain

CONCLUSION

Throughout this book, we have explored essential strategies and insights for navigating relationships impacted by trauma. Understanding trauma is foundational to providing empathetic support to our partners. We delved into the various types of trauma physical, emotional, and psychological and discussed their profound effects on individuals and their relationships. By recognizing the signs and symptoms of trauma, we equip ourselves to offer compassionate understanding and effective support. Central to our exploration is the theme of supporting our partners through empathy, communication, and unconditional support. We emphasized the importance of creating a safe and nurturing environment where our partners feel validated and understood. This involves understanding trauma responses and learning to set healthy boundaries that respect both our needs and those of our partners. Effective communication and empathy emerged as crucial pillars for fostering intimacy and mutual understanding amidst the challenges of trauma.

Rebuilding trust and ensuring emotional safety are essential steps in supporting our partner's healing journey. We explored practical strategies for rebuilding trust, such as consistency, transparency, and mutual respect. By creating a secure environment where our partners feel valued and respected, we lay the foundation for healing and growth within the relationship. Self-care emerged as a recurring theme throughout our discussion, underscoring the importance of maintaining our own well-being while supporting a loved one through trauma. We explored strategies for self-care, including seeking support networks and nurturing resilience. Recognizing that our own emotional and physical well-being strengthens our ability to support others, we emphasized the significance of prioritizing self-care as an act of compassion and sustainability.

In navigating relationship dynamics affected by trauma, we explored healthy practices for maintaining intimacy and resolving conflicts. Effective conflict resolution strategies, grounded in empathy and mutual respect, were highlighted as essential for fostering resilience and growth within the relationship. Maintaining a positive outlook and embracing resilience emerged as transformative attitudes that empower partners to navigate challenges with optimism and determination.

Finally, in our exploration of hope and moving forward, we celebrated the milestones achieved in healing and growth. We encouraged partners to embrace optimism as a guiding principle and to acknowledge progress as a testament to their resilience. The journey through trauma is marked by both challenges and moments of profound connection and growth. By celebrating each step forward and maintaining a hopeful outlook, partners can continue to nurture a relationship that is resilient, supportive, and filled with love.

To all readers embarking on this journey of supporting a partner through trauma, know that your efforts are significant and deeply meaningful. Your commitment to understanding, empathy, and growth is a testament to the strength of your relationship. Embrace each challenge as an opportunity for deeper connection and personal growth.

Remember to prioritize your own well-being and seek support when needed. Together, you can create a relationship that thrives despite adversity, grounded in love, resilience, and hope.

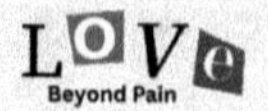
LOVe
Beyond Pain